THE SHAKERS

HISTORY, CULTURE, AND CRAFT

Lesley Herzberg

Curator, Hancock Shaker Village

Published in Great Britain in 2015 by Shire Publications Ltd, PO Box 883, Oxford, OX1 9PL, UK.

PO Box 3985, New York, NY 10185-3985, USA.

E-mail: shire@shirebooks.co.uk
www.shirebooks.co.uk

A CIP catalogue record for this book is available from the British Library.

Shire Library no. 813.   ISBN-13: 978 0 74781 462 7
PDF e-book ISBN: 978 1 78442 068 0
ePub ISBN: 978 1 78442 067 3

Hancock Shaker Village has asserted its right under the Copyright, Designs and Patents Act, 1988, to be identified as the author of this book.

Typeset in Garamond Pro and Gill Sans.

Printed in China through Worldprint Ltd.

14 15 16 17 18   10 9 8 7 6 5 4 3 2 1

COVER IMAGE
Cupboard and case of drawers, Mount Lebanon, NY, circa 1840. Pine and basswood, with yellow wash, brass latches, and iron hinges.

TITLE PAGE IMAGE
The 1854 gift drawing, *The Tree of Life,* by Hancock Believer and instrument Hannah Cohoon, is often reproduced.

CONTENTS PAGE IMAGE
Made around 1830, this Shaker blanket chest is simple and without ornament. Only the most basic elements are included, although the inclusion of a locked top compartment is interesting in a community where everything is shared.

AUTHOR ACKNOWLEDGMENTS
Several people supported me in the process of writing this book. Many thanks to my colleagues and the Board of Trustees at Hancock Shaker Village. Also thanks to: Starlyn D'Angelo, Michael Fredericks, Magda Gabor-Hotchkiss, Michael Graham, Christian Goodwillie, Jerry Grant, Brother Arnold Hadd, Gay Herzberg, Eric Korenman, Lisa Seymour, and Christine (Sze Hin) So. As always, thanks to my boys for your unconditional love—Matthew, Jacob, Henry, and of course, Calvin.

IMAGE ACKNOWLEDGMENTS
I would also like to thank the people and institutions who have allowed me to use illustrations, which are acknowledged as follows:

Michael Fredericks, page 3, 15 (all), 28, 29, 40, 44, 45 (top), 46 (top), 47 (bottom), 48 (bottom), 49 (left), 51 (all), 52 (all); Eric Korenman, page 26, 30, 31, 32; New York State Museum, Albany, New York, page 8; Shaker Heritage Society of Albany, New York, page 11 (top); Shaker Museum | Mount Lebanon, page 10, 18; United Society of Shakers, Sabbathday Lake, Maine, page 59 (all). All other images are from the collection of Hancock Shaker Village.

Shire Publications is supporting the Woodland Trust, the UK's leading woodland conservation charity, by funding the dedication of trees.

CONTENTS

THE ORIGINS OF THE SHAKERS

THE RELIGIOUS GROUP known as the Shakers arrived in America in 1774. Their proper name is the United Society of Believers in Christ's Second Appearing, or Believers for short. Their story, however, begins in England with a charismatic woman and her unfailing belief that God spoke directly and clearly to her.

Ann Lee was an illiterate factory worker in the industrial city of Manchester. Born on February 29, 1736, she and her family lived a working-class life on Toad Lane. She had a deeply religious mother and a father who was a blacksmith by trade. At a young age, Ann showed herself to be spiritually advanced: she had visions and communicated with God. She was forced to marry her father's apprentice, Abraham Stanley (sometimes called Standerin). The couple had four children, all of whom died in infancy. In this sad state of mind, Ann's vivid spiritual visions increased, enveloped her daily life, and caused her years of suffering.

Ann's search for spiritual answers led her to join a newly established religious group in Manchester that was practicing outside the strict confines of the Church of England. They primarily met in small groups at private homes, such as that of early group leaders James and Jane Wardley, and became known as the Wardley Society. The group had a variety of spiritual influences, including those of Quakers, Methodists, and French Prophets or Camisards. Their beliefs grew out of aspects adopted from this collection of traditions. The

Quakers practiced pacifism and individual spirit-led worship, and the Methodists also emphasized this form of personal practice. The influence of the French Prophets introduced an ecstatic form of physical worship, which was adopted by the Wardley Society, and the group became known to outsiders by the derisive term "Shaking Quakers", or "Shakers", for short.

It was clear that Ann was different from the rest of the group: her visions and charismatic presence set her apart. In 1770, she found the spiritual answer she had been seeking for so long—she had a revelation that her children's deaths were the result of the "unclean" union with her husband. She understood from these visions that the root of all sin began with Adam and Eve in the Garden of Eden. Their fall from grace condemned all of humanity to a life of sin. Therefore, the only way to regain an unblemished state was to practice celibacy, and refrain from all carnal knowledge. She believed that only by releasing ourselves from the attachments of this world, could we truly find a pure relationship with God.

Armed with this new understanding, Ann became the leader of the Wardley Society, and soon became known to all as Mother Ann. Although her influence is wide reaching, even today no known image of Mother Ann exists, although

Russel Casson & John Berry, *A Plan of the Towns of Manchester and Salford in the County Palatine of Lancaster*, about 1750, showing a detail of Toad Lane where Ann Lee grew up.

This image, titled *The Whirling Gift*, illustrates early Shaker "laboring" or dancing. Believers would spin in a frenzy, and then fall prostrate to the floor in exhaustion.

a follower, Polly Collins, created a likeness of her in a gift drawing (an image received in a vision). A physical description of Mother Ann was written long after her death by Rufus Bishop and Seth Youngs Wells, editors and compilers of the 1816 *Testimonies*, and provides some insight into her appearance:

MOTHER ANN LEE was a woman, in nature, of a strong constitution, rather exceeding the ordinary size of women; very straight and well proportioned in form, or rather thick; of a light complexion, and blue eyes; her hair of a light chestnut brown. In appearance, she was very majestic, and her countenance was such as inspired confidence and respect; and by many of the world, who saw her, without prejudice, she was called beautiful. To her faithful children, she appeared to possess a degree of dignified beauty and heavenly love transcending that of mortals.

Dissenting religious sects were persecuted in Manchester, and the early Shakers did not escape this fate. Members were often chased through the streets and thrown in jail. Mother Ann and her followers were imprisoned and beaten for interrupting church services and preaching publicly about their new and seemingly strange religion.

After 1770, James Whittaker, a follower of Mother Ann, had his own personal vision: it was America. In *Ann Lee, A Biography* by Frederick W. Evans, Whittaker wrote, "I saw a large tree, every leaf of which shone with such brightness as made it appear like a burning torch, representing the Church of Christ which will yet be established in this land."

Soon after James Whittaker recounted his vision to the group, Mother Ann and eight followers sailed for the

This detail from *An Emblem of the Heavenly Sphere*, by Polly Collins in 1854, is one of the only known depictions of Mother Ann Lee.

Hannah Cohoon, *The Tree of Light or Blazing Tree*, 1845. This gift drawing, made at Hancock, Massachusetts, may represent James Whittaker's vision that encouraged the Shakers to travel to America.

John Montresor,
Map of the
Province of New
York, 1775. This
map depicts the
state of New
York after the
Shakers arrived
in America. It
also details
the Manor of
Rensselaerswyck,
where the
Shakers leased
land that was
soon to become
Watervliet.

United States. It was known to be a land of religious freedom and opportunity. Their ship, the *Mariah*, cleared customs in New York on August 5, 1774 and the group disembarked on August 6. They found odd jobs in the city to support themselves. One of the Believers journeyed north up the Hudson River to Niskayuna, located northwest of Albany, New York. Here, the group was able to lease property from the Dutch patroon Kiliaen van Rensselaer, who owned large parcels of land.

Niskayuna became known as Watervliet and was established as the first Shaker settlement in America. Mother Ann was able to join the small group that had assembled there by the winter of 1776. The Shakers kept to themselves during their early years in America, as the Revolutionary War played out around them. Hardship continued to follow the group, even in this promised land. Their living conditions were poor, and the Believers were crowded into a small house and sometimes went without proper sustenance. The land they leased was mostly swamps, and converting it to farmland was difficult work. They were often suspected of being British spies or sympathizers, and Mother Ann was jailed in Albany along with some of her followers for preaching pacifism. To outsiders, this strange new religious community who separated themselves from the world and followed a female leader was cause for concern during a time of social and political upheaval in the British colonies.

The strenuous economic and social conditions caused by the Revolutionary War led to unrest and uncertainty among settlers in the northeast. This tenuous time set the stage for the Shakers and their message, which offered a clear path to salvation. Congregationalists and Baptists were already swept up in the New Light Revival of 1779, which was centered along the New York and Massachusetts border. New Lights were seeking a direct connection with the divine and assurance of their salvation. As this revival waned in early 1780, former participants became aware of the Shakers and began to travel to Niskayuna to meet with Mother Ann and her followers. After several months of visiting back and forth, many New Lights became convinced of the Shaker message. This resulted in many conversions for the growing society; sometimes even large portions of established congregations would join together as their ministers came to believe in the Shakers' teachings.

The so-called "Dark Day" that occurred on May 19, 1780 was seen as a sign that the Day of Judgment had arrived. The skies across New England darkened for a full day, caused by smoke from a large forest fire in Canada. This led to a fearful period where many people turned to religion for answers— the Shakers responded to this atmospheric event by opening their gospel in America.

Mother Ann and her missionaries preached all over the northeast, attracting converts along the way. They endured many hardships on their journeys: they were often beaten, thrown in prison, and chased out of towns by mobs. These experiences took their toll on the Shaker leader's health,

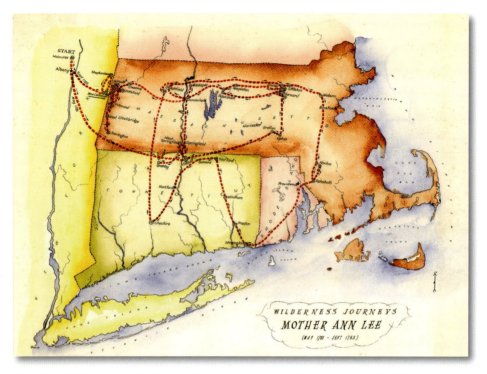

WILDERNESS JOURNEYS
MOTHER ANN LEE
(MAY 1781 – SEPT 1783)

Dr P. Ross Teller, Wilderness Journeys (of) Mother Ann Lee (May 1781–Sept 1783), 1952.

and after only ten years on American soil, Mother Ann died in 1784 and was buried with fellow Believers at the Niskayuna settlement.

Even after Mother Ann's death, the Shaker movement grew and flourished. Those passionate followers that inherited the fledgling society believed in their cause and guided the Believers to great prominence. Father James Whittaker held the society together until 1787, when Father Joseph Meacham emerged as the leader and chose Mother Lucy Wright as his female counterpart to lead the Ministry. Often referred to as the "First Parents," Father Joseph and Mother Lucy were American-born converts who gathered the scattered societies together. The Shakers' "Parent Ministry" was based at Mount Lebanon, New York, after Mother Ann's death. The Shakers' hierarchy began to take shape at this time, with the Parent Ministry overseeing all communities and each individual village also guided by two Elders and two Eldresses acting as Ministers. In addition, the norms of behavior within Shaker communities were established during this period, and in time these were codified in written form, called the *Millennial Laws*. These were a set of rules that would guide Believers in their spiritual and temporal lives, and provide the basis for Shaker life for years to come.

Mother Ann's grave in the cemetery at the Watervliet community, now the Shaker Heritage Society, near Albany. The headstone has been replaced at least once.

After the founding of Watervliet, nearly two dozen more Shaker communities were established in America—some closing quickly after they were gathered, and some lasting a century or more. They reached as far west as Indiana and as far south as Florida. At their height in the mid-nineteenth century, the Shakers claimed approximately five thousand members.

This stereoview of the Mount Lebanon community shows the extent of land and buildings during the late nineteenth century in the thriving center of the Shaker world.

Irving, Photographer - Troy.

SHAKER THEOLOGY AND RELIGIOUS PRACTICE

THE SHAKERS ARE a Christian Millennialist group. They often refer to themselves as the Millennial Church, or the Manifestation of the Second Coming, which they believe had already taken place through Mother Ann. Shakers believe in the dual nature of God, often referred to by the term "dual Godhead." As a spirit, God is both male and female. Mother Ann was imbued with the Christ Spirit as were many Believers after her. For the Shakers, this event represents the second coming of Jesus, not in the flesh but in the spirit. In the *Testimonies* of 1816, Mother Ann said, "It is not I that speaks; it is the Christ that dwells in me."

Believers are required to confess their sins to the Shaker Ministry, or leadership. Brothers confess to Elders, and sisters confess to Eldresses. In this way, Shakers cleanse their souls of imperfections each day and at special times throughout the year, allowing them to be closer to God.

Shakers practice communal living and property ownership. New converts are considered novitiates and enter a trial period to see if Shaker life is right for them. After this period, novitiates can make the choice to sign the Shaker covenant and turn their property over to the community. The covenant is a legal document that commits the signer as a full member of the Church, with all the benefits that come with membership. All property is held communally, and all members receive the same benefits, making the Shakers one of the first groups to practice equality between races and genders.

Polly Collins, *An Emblem of the Heavenly Sphere*, 1854 (see pages 22–3).

GROUP OF SHAKERS.

This stereoview of the North Family Ministry at Mount Lebanon about 1875, shows Eldresses Anna White and Antoinette Doolittle, and Elders Frederick Evans and Daniel Offord. The Shakers believe in equality of the sexes, and their leadership model reflects this principle.

Communal life for the Shakers means living together in large dwelling houses, with men and women under the same roof. Unlike many other celibate monastic orders, Shakers do not separate the sexes. Men and women may enter the Church as a married couple, but upon signing the covenant, they become spiritual brother and sister. They then live together as a communal family, with adults separated from children, and brethren and sisters having their own workshops and trades.

Father Joseph Meacham established what the Shakers refer to as "gospel order," as a way of gathering and maintaining Believers. Shaker villages were divided into specific "families," with each family made up of between forty and fifty members. Families had their own dwelling houses, barns, and workshops. Shaker villages often included North, South, East, and West Families, according to their geographical location, and Second Families. These were all organized around the central or "Church" Family where the community Meetinghouse was located. Usually one of these outlying families was a "gathering" or "novitiate" order where people could live during their trial period before fully converting. These villages were an attempt by the Shakers to separate themselves from the "World"—as they referred to

The Brick Dwelling at Hancock Shaker Village, Pittsfield, Massachusetts, was built in 1830. Its unique architecture reflects the Shakers' belief in communal living, as well as separation of the sexes, in order to preserve their vow of celibacy.

The Brethren's Shop at Hancock is a mirror image of the Sisters' Dairy & Weave Shop, and housed the trades and crafts produced by the Shaker brothers. Brethren's and sisters' work was viewed as equally valuable to the community.

The Sisters' Dairy & Weave Shop at Hancock housed the trades and crafts produced by the Shaker sisters. It is a mirror image of the Brethren's Shop. The buildings are similar so that one gender is not elevated above another.

those outside the faith—and to create a veritable heaven on earth. Only elevated members called Trustees were appointed to deal with business and legal matters with the world outside their gates.

Removing their members from the temptations of the world helped to foster a key concept of the Shakers— "union"—which means being spiritually bound together while living in community. A Shaker strives to find union with oneself, other members of the church, and ultimately, with God. Union can also mean being "gathered in" or joining the community. This concept is so central to the Shaker faith that several Shaker villages had the word "union" as part of their name, such as Union Village, Ohio; South Union, Kentucky; and West Union, Indiana.

Shakers practice pacifism—all are God's creatures, they believe, and should be treated with kindness and respect. "Do unto others as you would have done unto you" is a teaching that the Shakers live by every day. After the Revolutionary War, many soldiers joined the ranks of Believers. The Parent Ministry at Mount Lebanon discouraged them from collecting their military pensions from the American government, as it was money that was essentially earned through wartime activities, and the Shaker communities did not wish to accept these funds. At the beginning of the Civil War in 1861, Shakers were recognized as conscientious objectors by President Abraham Lincoln, and were exempted from service. In thanks, the Shakers sent the president one of their now-famous rocking chairs. Although the Shakers did not support wars, they supported the soldiers fighting in them, and often sent clothing or medical supplies to those suffering from the effects of war.

Shaker worship services consist of singing, dancing, Biblical readings, and personal testimonies. In the late eighteenth and early nineteenth centuries, a Shaker meeting would involve a type of spiritual trance, in which Believers would spin and

The Whirling Gift, detail of an exhausted Shaker dancer.

dance in a frenzy, as if possessed by the spirit. In 1848, David R. Lamson wrote *Two Years' Experience Among the Shakers*. Lamson was an apostate (one who left the church) and sought to clarify the seeming mysteries behind the Shaker faith for worldly readers. He describes a Shaker meeting and the ecstatic dancing that took place: "All this time the young sisters continue their turning so swiftly … but they must not be checked in their gifts, for it is by the inspiration of God, that all these things are done. They often fall prostrate on the floor, and all animation seems lost for a season."

As Shaker meetings became more scripted, these frenetic movements turned into choreographed dances that involved singing, marching, hand gestures, and stomping. The Shakers sing and dance in order to praise God, drawing their inspiration from King David during his entrance into Jerusalem. In the King James Version of the Bible it states, "And David danced before the Lord with all his might." (2 Samuel 6:14). There are no ministers in a Shaker service, and there is no central podium or pulpit. All Believers are graced with the Christ Spirit, so all are free to speak and testify as the spirit moves them. Testimonies are followed by songs, and the meeting comes to a close when Believers are finished speaking. Around 1880, one of the longest meetings on record was noted in a Hancock journal by simply stating, "Good meeting. 22 hours."

This image appeared in *Frank Leslie's Illustrated Newspaper* about 1873. Inside the 1824 Meetinghouse at Mount Lebanon, brethren and sisters are in separate circles but are dancing together, while observers from the World line the built-in benches. Shakers welcomed visitors to their meetings in the hope that they would gain converts.

Over one thousand manuscript hymnals survive, containing tens of thousands of Shaker songs. Believers developed a form of written music called letteral notation, using only the letters that correspond to the individual notes. Some songs were unique and received in visions, and others borrowed tunes from folk songs and Shakers changed the words for their own spiritual purposes. In the early days of the faith the songs used vocables—sounds such as "lo, lo, lo"—in both fast and exceedingly slow tempos, which expressed a spiritual connection without the use of words. The Believers would experience a possession of the spirit that outwardly manifested itself in music and movement. Songs communicated Mother Ann's trials and tribulations, and spoke of the healing power of faith.

The song "Stone Prison" dates from 1842, when a follower in Harvard, Massachusetts, wrote, "This song Mother Ann sang through an instrument at the table when the Family was eating bread and water." ("An instrument" refers to the receiver of the song.) "I Never Did Believe" was written in 1829, and attributed to Eldress Betsy Bates of Mount Lebanon.

STONE PRISON

How can I but love my dear faithful children
Who are willing to bear and suffer with me
When I was on earth and in a cold prison
I cried to my God to remember poor me

I NEVER DID BELIEVE

I never did believe that I ever could be saved
Without giving up all to God
So I freely give the whole
My body and my soul
To the Lord God Amen

Just as Shaker dance took on a more scripted feel in the mid-nineteenth century, Shaker music followed suit. Songs that had been passed down in oral traditions were finally written down. Shakers even made writing pens with which to draw musical staff (the five horizontal lines and four spaces on which music is written), to give order and precision to the music recorded on the page. The Shakers published a wide variety of hymnals. The earliest was printed at Hancock in

This hymnal demonstrates the Shakers' use of letteral notation.

1813 and titled *Millennial Praises*. The most widely recognized Shaker song is "Simple Gifts," which was borrowed by Aaron Copeland for his Appalachian Spring suite and for a hymn called "Lord of the Dance," among many others.

> ### SIMPLE GIFTS
> 'Tis the gift to be simple, 'tis a gift to be free
> 'Tis the gift to come down where you ought to be
> And when you find yourself in the place just right
> 'Twill be in the valley of love and delight

Beginning in August 1837, the Shakers entered a period of religious revival, which they referred to as either the "Era of Manifestations" or "Mother's Work." Those Believers who had known Mother Ann personally were passing on, and new Believers needed to find a way to reconnect with the original messages of Shakerism. This period saw a great deal of excitement and religious fervor in the communities, and each Shaker community received a spiritual name during this time.

Believers crafted staff writing pens to standardize their music, making it easier to read.

Hancock was "City of Peace," Mount Lebanon was "Holy Mount," and Watervliet was "Wisdom's Valley," for example.

In favorable weather, outdoor mountain meetings took place at special locations. Each community had Believers who were divinely inspired to consecrate a piece of land and designate it as a "feast ground." Here they would hold meetings surrounding the "fountain stone." The feast was a spiritual one, and the fountain offered the "water of life" for the Believers. Brethren and sisters would march up the mountain singing, arriving at the cleared feast ground, and gather around the fountain stone. In Lamson's *Two Years' Experience Among the Shakers* he recounts, "These meetings on the mountain are designed to be very free and lively, and, also very impressive. It is a time for the special outpouring of Spiritual gifts."

One product of the Era of Manifestations was the spiritual gifts that were sent to Believers. "Instruments" would receive messages and translate them into poems, songs, or drawings. Shaker "gift drawings" are among the most hauntingly beautiful works of American folk art known today. Created by

Mountain Meeting, from Lamson's *Two Years' Experience Among the Shakers*, depicts an outdoor meeting at Hancock's Mount Sinai. Outdoor meetings were closed to people from the World, and such illustrations served to explain these mysterious ceremonies. The Shakers hold their hands as if to shake out their sins physically.

Image taken in 1897 of the fountain stone in situ at the Shaker community in Shirley, Massachusetts. After the end of the Era of Manifestations, many communities buried or destroyed their fountain stones in order to keep the teachings within the confines of the Church. Some have been located, but many are still missing.

untrained artists who were mostly women, these works of art are ethereal, and contained messages from Mother Ann and the male and female aspects of the Godhead, known as Heavenly Father and Holy Mother Wisdom. They depict elements from the natural world, as well as images from Christian iconography. Their bright colors belie the commonly held notion that Shakers were a dour, straitlaced group. They are joyful visions of a world the Shakers believe is yet to come.

Hannah Cohoon was an instrument at the Hancock community. Her gift drawings have a bold, natural style that showed a great love of color. Her best-known work is the most frequently reproduced Shaker gift drawing, *The Tree of Life*. The text underneath it seems to be an afterthought for folk-art lovers, yet it is the text that tells us of the real importance of the tree:

CITY OF PEACE Monday July 3rd 1854. I received a draft of a beautiful Tree penciled on a large sheet of white paper bearing ripe fruit. I saw it plainly; it looked very singular to me. I have since learned that this tree grows in the Spirit Land. Afterwards the spirit show'd me plainly the branches, leaves and fruit, painted or drawn upon paper. The leaves were check'd or cross'd and the same colors you see here. I entreated Mother Ann to tell me the name of this tree: which she did Oct. 1st 4th hour P.M. by moving the hand of a medium to write twice over Your Tree is The Tree of Life. Seen and painted by Hannah Cohoon. Age 66.

Polly Collins was another Believer at Hancock. She was a prolific instrument and was responsible for sixteen known gift drawings. In *An Emblem of the Heavenly Sphere* (see page 12) she provides portraits of individuals, Shakers and non-Shakers alike. Mother Ann Lee appears in the top row of faces along with Father James Whittaker and Father William Lee, her brother. Also in the top row is Christopher Columbus, whose discovery of America resulted in a land of religious freedom of which the Shakers took full advantage. A portrait labeled "The Savior" represents Jesus Christ, whose placement is significant in that he sits directly underneath the image of Mother Ann, representing the Shakers' ultimate belief in their founder above all others. Jesus is dressed in Shaker clothing, and has his hair cut like the rest of the brethren. The only aspect that sets him apart is that his hands are raised, perhaps in a gesture of blessing. Mother Ann's arms are raised as well, most likely in a gesture of supplication.

Other portraits include Christian heroes and heroines, such as Saint Peter, Queen Esther, Moses, and the Virgin Mary. Men and women stand as equals—those who have played a part in Christian history, and paved the way for the Shakers and their message of the second coming of Christ.

Polly Collins also describes the spiritual rewards that await Believers in heaven: "Rejoice, go on, you'l yet obtain the sight, an entrance in those regions of delight. Your praise will mingle with the happy throng, and to their holy circle, you'l belong." She also speaks of the "Holy Two in One", referring to the Shakers' belief in a dual Godhead. In addition, she provides several small scenes along with the images of trees and flowers that surround the portraits. In one, a guardian angel inhabits what appears to be a Shaker room: a Shaker straight chair and writing desk sit by her side, and a clock on the wall keeps time. In another scene, Collins depicts the parting of the Red Sea, illustrating a miracle that occurred to save the Israelites in their time of need. The Shakers viewing this gift drawing are meant to make the connection that unfailing belief in God will save all those who are righteous.

A Trumpet from Moses, to reveal the word of God to the Nations

A Necklace from the Woman of Samaria

A type of Joseph's lamps that lighted him thro' the wilderness of woe during his refreshments for the time he was rejected by his brethren, and when he was called to battle they gave him light by night and supported him by day.

Those who partake of this shall be crowned in Eternity fruit with glory

Thus saith Holy Wisdom. I too child of Her peculiar care. In my Wisdom beloved little one from you the choicest of your fruit shall soon be gathered. I have noticed glorification which shall of your hands gain to you be a gain to very beautiful. in eternity your deeds

My dearly loved ones to be taken a season. And a lasting recommendation

A fan of Mother Hannah's to blow away buffetings: The cruelest of foes.

Come unto Me, saith Wisdom in thy infancy Devote thy whole heart to serve thy Creator in the morning of thy days and of the beautiful treasures of my Kingdom children shall.

A dove of Peace.

Upon the Mountain of fruits of every kind, planted & chosen kindred, tongue that my blessing

my pleasure saith the And from and them will seed in the hearts of some and people. There are none may reach them. I will Trumpet & the sound thereof shall reach their ears and I will send loud to sus= tain their souls.

A steadfast mind Like flowers of Peace yields fragrance pure and sublime.

A type of Hannah's kerchiefs, by Father Mother pocket-hand Drawn James for Jane Blanchard 1854

Within the drawing:

A Cage of singing birds from Sarah of old.

A Dove of Purity.

I placed

Polly Jane Reed, *A Type of Mother Hannah's Pocket Handkerchief*, 1851. This gift drawing illustrates the variety of colors and aspects from the natural world that were often depicted in these spiritual revelations.

FORM FOLLOWS FAITH: WORK AS WORSHIP

THE MEETINGHOUSE IS the center of the Shakers' spiritual world, although worship is not limited to the confines of that building. Work is a form of worship for the Shakers, so they praise God in all that they do, from milking a cow to weaving a rug. According to the *Testimonies* of 1816, Mother Ann once said, "Put your hands to work and your heart to God." These lyrics are from a Shaker song that is sung by sisters as they work at the spinning wheel:

> ROUND AROUND, MOTHER's blessing goes round
> Round the world around
> Twisting strands of love and union
> Into life's eternal blessed
> Mother's hand is on the spindle
> Turning us to peace and rest

It helps them keep track of the yarn skein and pass the time, always keeping the spinner's mind on the true purpose of her work—that the fruits of her labor are for the glory of God.

In the late eighteenth and early nineteenth centuries, Shakers created objects for use within their own communities. Many objects were made for the general Shaker population, while some were fashioned with particular recipients in mind. If a certain brother was very tall, he might have a higher chair made especially for him by a woodworker. If another brother

These spinning wheels are exhibited in the Brick Dwelling at Hancock.

These trousers were made for a brother who had outgrown them. Instead of making him a new pair, which would be considered wasteful, the sisters added a drawstring to the back panel.

was getting a bit too thick around the middle, the sisters who mended clothes would add a lace to the back of his trousers that could be taken in and let out as needed. These special articles were made with care by fellow Believers.

Shakers were readily able to meet the supply and demand for goods in their small villages. If an object was required, it was made to order. There was no assembly line to keep up with, and no quota to reach each day. Shakers could go to their workshops and take the time to make a good-quality article with the best materials. Good work would need to be replaced less often, saving time and industry in the long run. In the 1816 *Testimonies* Mother Ann is quoted as saying, "Do all your work as though you had a thousand years to live, and as though you were going to die tomorrow."

In the true spirit of Shaker union, some objects the Believers produced required the expertise of brethren and sisters working together. Coming together in union was a Shaker principle, and a basis for true community life. The union found in work meant creating products that equally used the strengths of each sex in order to produce a whole that represented the community. Many of the traditional-gendered labor roles from the outside world were also observed in Shaker villages: men performed heavy agricultural and construction duties, while women cleaned and mostly handled the cooking. However, traditional labor roles were blurred in Shaker communities when brethren and sisters worked together on different aspects of a product. At Hancock, the brethren made yarn swifts which the sisters painted, and as part of the herbal industry, especially at Mount Lebanon, the brethren made the extracts while the sisters bottled, labeled, and packed them for shipping.

Believers' work was simple and without ornament. The embellishments of the World were of no use to the Shakers— they took extra time and materials to produce, and reflected a vanity in the user as well as in the maker. Craftsmen and women might be accused of flaunting a special skill that would serve to set them apart from the rest of their brethren and sisters. For this reason, Shakers dressed alike, wore their hair alike, and had similar chairs, looms, or lathes in order to create and preserve equality among the entire community.

Objects were made to reflect God's creation, and their makers strove for nothing less than perfection in their products. In Edward and Faith Andrews' *Religion in Wood: A Book of Shaker Furniture*, Trappist monk Thomas Merton wrote that "the peculiar grace of a Shaker chair is due to the fact that it was made by someone capable of believing that an angel might come and sit on it." As much as Shakers praised God with song and dance, they also praised God with the creations from their hands.

The Shaker chair represents the innovative spirit, design aesthetic, and marketing prowess of the Believers.

SHAKERS AS ENTREPRENEURS: SELLING TO THE WORLD

A FTER THE SHAKERS had outfitted their own villages sufficiently, they had the workforce and the resources to begin producing a surplus of goods. This surplus was to be sold to the outside World.

Communities produced a wide range of products for sale. Packaged seeds, brooms, chairs, rug whips, yarn swifts, wool cards, cloaks, herbal medicines, sewing boxes, candied nuts, and sweaters are just a few examples of Shaker products. There was some overlap of items, but the Shakers made sure that one village was not invading any other village's sales districts.

The Shaker Ministry appointed Office Deacons, or Trustees, to handle all business with the World. These were reliable men and women who had proven themselves within the community, and were then trained by their predecessors to interact with those outside of their insular villages. They were known to be honest in their dealings, and were responsible for marketing Shaker products and handling the exchange of monies. It was the Trustee who had their initials on Shaker products and packaging, so that the buyer had a specific name to attach to a product and not simply a group of unknown people. Shakers soon developed a reputation for high-quality products at reasonable prices.

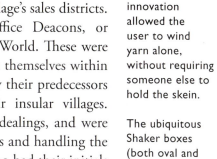

Opposite: A yarn swift, sometimes called a table swift. This Shaker innovation allowed the user to wind yarn alone, without requiring someone else to hold the skein.

The ubiquitous Shaker boxes (both oval and round versions) were produced by the brethren, while the sisters outfitted them with sewing essentials. This box was sold by the Mount Lebanon Shakers in the 1920s.

Shaker cloaks were made for children and adults, and became fashionable in the nineteenth century. The cloaks worn by Shaker sisters were more muted in color than those sold to the World.

In 1808, in *An Historical Sketch of the County of Berkshire*, Thomas Allen, a Congregational Minister from Pittsfield, Massachusetts, described the Hancock Shakers as "very harmless, innocent people, good citizens, and honest, industrious, peaceable members of society. They are good farmers and artists, and offer nothing for sale that is deceptive."

The Shaker garden seed industry began in the late eighteenth century. Both the Mount Lebanon and Watervliet communities claim to have originated this lucrative business. Most farms at this time were producing vegetables on a large scale, and farmers would buy seeds in bulk. The Shakers were the first to put their seeds into small packages (called papers) so that the average person could plant a small

Seed packets, or papers as the Shakers called them, were printed by the communities. The initials here refer to Hancock Trustees Daniel Goodrich Junior, and David Terry.

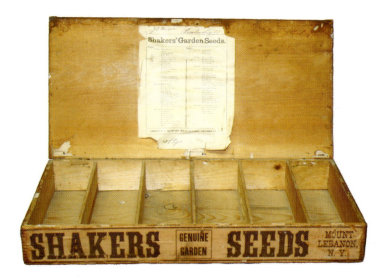

Shaker seed boxes were an early form of marketing, and served to make the Shaker products readily identifiable to customers.

Seed lists were another way to make buyers aware of Shaker products. Broadsides, such as this one produced by the Shakers at Hancock in 1821, were widely distributed.

kitchen garden. Shakers would place the seed packets into wooden boxes with colorful advertising on the lid, bring these boxes to small country stores in the spring, and collect money from the proprietor in the fall when they took the boxes home to be refilled. Shaker Trustees or another trusted Believer or agent would travel on established seed routes throughout their region.

The materials that survive from the Shaker seed industry largely come from Mount Lebanon and Watervliet, New York; Hancock and Shirley, Massachusetts; Enfield, New Hampshire; and South Union, Kentucky.

The Shakers often printed their own marketing materials, which were widely distributed. The design of seed lists, broadsides, packages, and box lids grew increasingly sophisticated when the Shakers began to hire printers to produce multicolored lithographs. Advertising labels progressed from the simple seed packet to the more colorful and

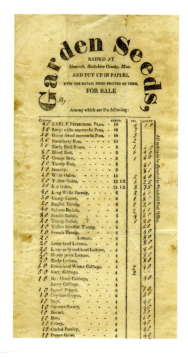

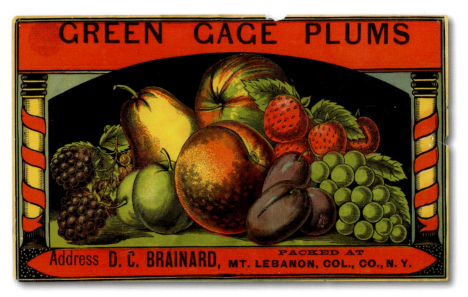

GREEN GAGE PLUMS

Address **D. C. BRAINARD**, MT. LEBANON, COL., CO., N. Y. PACKED AT

The Mount Lebanon Shakers produced this advertising label for their greengage plums in the 1890s.

complex poster—the Shakers had to compete with fellow seed companies or sacrifice the generous income seed sales produced.

The Shaker aesthetic and the disdain for superfluous decoration was a part of the "classic" period of Shaker design (1820–1840). In the later nineteenth century, the Shakers embraced Victorian tastes in order to appear relevant and contemporary to potential converts and customers. Always progressive thinkers and innovators, Shaker furniture, architecture, and advertising, among others, took on more modern decoration.

Shaker chairs were continually made for use within their villages, but the communities soon saw

Brother George O. Donnell's patent for his chair-tilter device. Shakers sought patents for their inventions and improvements, and Believers held over three hundred patents in the eighteenth and nineteenth centuries.

the market need for side chairs and rocking chairs. The straight-back or ladder-back chair was common throughout the northeastern United States ever since settlers began to arrive in the seventeenth century, bringing their European furniture along with them to the new world. The Shakers redesigned the ladder-back chair. They canted the entire chair frame backwards and slightly splayed the back posts to provide the sitter with a more comfortable back position. They made their chairs with a variety of seating types—cane, splint, or woven webbing. The chairs could have arms and rockers or neither of these features. They came in a variety of sizes—No. 0 would fit a small child, and No. 7 was a large chair for a tall man. The Shakers invented a tilting device that fitted into the back posts, and prevented wear to the floor and to the chair itself. A Shaker brother named George O. Donnell even patented a metal version of the chair tilter in 1852.

Trustee Robert M. Wagan successfully ran the chair business at the Mount Lebanon community. In an effort to market his product, he opened a chair showroom in the factory to entice visitors to buy directly from the source.

Several Shaker villages made chairs for sale, but only one community had a dedicated chair factory. The Mount Lebanon Shakers produced and sold chairs in their village from 1789 until 1942. Several Trustees ran the chair business at that village, but one in particular stands out: Elder Robert M. Wagan (1833–1883). A savvy businessman, Wagan operated under the name R. M. Wagan & Co., and used broadsides and catalogs to market and sell Shaker chairs in the World. Shaker chairs were carried on consignment at regional furniture stores, and the business was so brisk that a new factory was built at Mount Lebanon's South Family in 1872. Many competing companies used the name "Shaker"

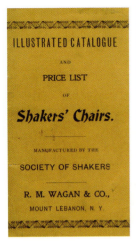
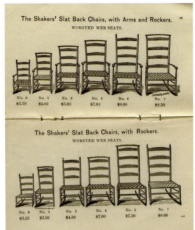

Several versions of Mount Lebanon Shaker chair catalogs were produced in the nineteenth century.

to sell their own chairs, capitalizing on the Shakers' marketing campaigns and reputation, so the Shakers began to add gold transfer labels to their chairs to certify them as genuine Shaker articles.

While many Shaker goods were sold by Trustees who traveled into the World on established routes, the Shakers welcomed those outside of their communities to enter their

These gold transfer labels were applied to rockers and wrapped around stretchers, and certified that the chair was a genuine Shaker product.

The interior of the Sisters' Shop at Hancock, about 1930. Note the modern convenience of linoleum on the floor alongside the traditional Shaker peg rails on the walls.

This image shows the Sisters' Shop at Hancock, about 1930. The shop faces the road to provide easy access for visitors. This building was torn down by the Shakers in 1958 to avoid paying taxes on an unused structure.

gates and shop at their sisters' shops or stores. While these stores were often located within the village's Trustees' Office, some were to be found in a sisters' shop that had an entrance on the main road. After 1860, these shops sold a variety of Shaker wares often referred to as "fancy work" or "fancy goods" that were made by the sisters. These items included sewing boxes, pincushions, pen wipes, brushes, doll clothing,

Each community had its own specific weave pattern of poplarware, and collectors use it to identify items with neither stamp nor label.

cloaks, small braided rugs, chair cushions, spool holders, and a variety of other small handmade objects.

In another instance of cooperation between the genders, Shaker sisters depended on the brethren to produce wooden carriers, either oval or round, and they would outfit them as sewing boxes by adding a silk interior with a needle case, pincushion, and an emery in the shape of a strawberry for sharpening needles. Also included was a small amount of beeswax. In addition, sisters also wove delicate poplar wood to create a product called poplarware. The brothers cut and sawed the poplar trees, and the sisters wove the strips on special looms. They then pasted the poplar strips onto paper and cotton cloth, to create poplar cloth that could be cut into various shapes. Sisters fitted the poplar cloth around wooden molds, then cut around the molds to make a variety of poplarware items.

Shaker sisters also produced cloaks that became fashionable

This silk bookmark was a marketing piece for the Mount Lebanon Shakers. Successful Shaker enterprises often took on the name of the Trustee who oversaw the production. Emma J. Neale ran the cloak business in the early twentieth century.

in the nineteenth and early twentieth centuries. Women from the World saw Shaker sisters wearing long cloaks and desired the warm, woolen outwear. Orders began to come in to the Shaker village at Canterbury, New Hampshire, where Eldress Dorothy Durgin created a design around 1890. From then on, all Shaker cloaks have been known as Dorothy cloaks. At Mount Lebanon, the cloak industry flourished in the late 1880s under Sister Clarissa Jacobs, and after 1899 under Trustee Emma J. Neale. The sisters themselves wore cloaks in conservative colors, while the cloaks made to order for women outside the community were in bright hues such as pink, red, cornflower blue, and purple. They were made in adult as well as children's sizes, and even dolls could be outfitted in Shaker cloaks. One famous customer was First Lady Frances Folsom Cleveland, who wore a gray Shaker cloak to Grover Cleveland's second presidential inauguration in 1893.

Hancock Sister Anna Delcheff models a Shaker cloak, about 1920.

This label is sewn into a child's bright red Dorothy cloak, and was most likely a product that was sold to the World.

ARCHITECTURE, FURNITURE, AND CRAFT

THE EXPRESSION OF Shaker beliefs and religious practice can be found in their architecture as well as in their material culture. These are physical manifestations of spiritual principles, not simply objects or structures that remain in museums as a part of American heritage. Examined closely, these pieces tell the stories of the Believers that crafted them and why their importance has outlived their makers.

One of the most iconic structures built by Shakers is the Round Stone Barn at Hancock. Constructed in 1826, it remains an architectural marvel, and demonstrates Shaker innovation and the importance of farming for Shaker communities. The Shakers combined and improved upon the established building forms of the round barn and bank barn. Bank barns were built into a hillside to allow easy access for wagons and livestock. The sheer scale of the Round Stone Barn is unique, as small family farms would not have needed such a large structure. The dairy operations in Shaker communities necessitated large barns, and the construction of the Round Stone Barn resulted in a highly successful dairy business at Hancock.

The barn was originally designed with two levels: the ground-floor cattle level, and the second- floor wagon level, with a cupola that topped a conical roof. The barn's circular form increased its overall efficiency. Hay wagons could enter the barn from a ramp, unload into the central haymow, and continue without having to turn around. On the cattle level,

After scientific paint analysis, the woodwork in this retiring room at Hancock was restored to its original chrome yellow and red lead color scheme.

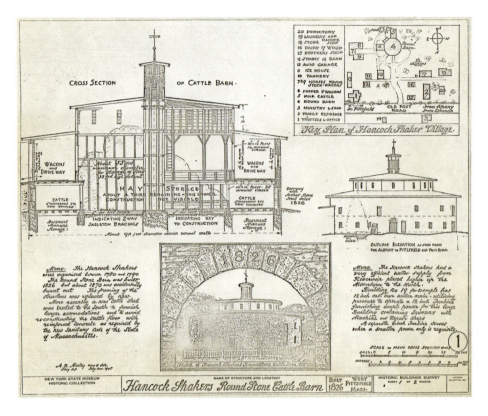

This drawing of the layout of Hancock's Round Stone Barn was prepared for the US government as part of the Historic American Buildings Survey in 1945.

fifty-two cows could stand with their heads in stanchions, facing a central ring, and a single farmer could feed and milk them quickly and efficiently.

When a fire devastated the structure in 1864, the Shakers saw it as an opportunity to improve the building—they embraced advances in technology with an eye to improving performance and efficiency. The building campaign started in 1866, with the addition of a flat monitor roof and cupola. Around 1870, a clerestory level was added to give the farmer more headroom, and to increase the light and airflow in order to prevent future fires. A manure level was also added at this time. The manure could be deposited through trap doors into this lower level, where a wagon could collect a load, and transport it out to nearby gardens to fertilize the soil.

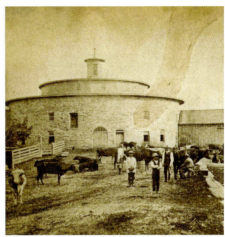

The Shakers lived communally, and their dwellings reflected this aspect of their belief system. In the early days after their arrival in America, the Believers lived in small farmhouses of converts, which was not ideal for the growing society who shared food, work, and worship together. As the communities began to thrive, they undertook major building campaigns to construct large dormitories or dwelling houses. These structures physically represent the Shaker ideal of separate but equal lives for brethren and sisters. The Brick Dwelling at Hancock was built in 1830 and is a mirror image from one side to the other. An invisible line down the center of the building separates the brothers on the east from the sisters on the west. Separate staircases, rooms, and doors ensured that the opposite sexes would not interact and thus tempt impure thoughts. Wide hallways discouraged brushing up against one another, even by accident. However, there were still communal spaces within the building where the brethren and sisters could be together. The dining room and meeting room were shared spaces, although the sexes kept to their designated sides even in these large rooms. The large kitchen in the basement and the two attic levels were primarily the domain of the sisters, as they did the cooking and cleaning, and accessed the storage spaces.

Left: This view of Round Stone Barn shows the second roof, built after the 1864 fire.

Right: Another view of the Round Stone Barn after 1883 when the clerestory level was added and the renovations were complete. Also shown are the Shaker brethren and their herd of cattle—a valuable resource for the Hancock community.

The Brick Dwelling at Hancock was built in 1830. The Shakers moved several buildings in the Church Family in order to accommodate the large structure.

The Meetinghouse was the center of the Shaker community's spiritual life. Believers from outlying families would gather every Sunday at the Church Family to worship together at this important building. Many Shaker Meetinghouses were based on a design by Moses Johnson, a brother at the Shaker village in Enfield, New Hampshire. The Meetinghouses were simple clapboard structures with a gambrel roof, doors for Believers at each side, and doors for people of the World facing the road. Separate staircases at each side of the building led to upstairs rooms for resident and visiting Ministry members.

The Meetinghouses at the New York Shaker communities of Mount Lebanon and Watervliet were larger and of a different design than the early Shaker Meetinghouses built in New England. Both had replaced their original Meetinghouses with larger structures, in order to accommodate the greater numbers of Believers, as well as the growing number of curious visitors from the World.

Mount Lebanon's second Meetinghouse, built in 1824, is an icon of Shaker architecture. It features a curved roof and had tiered seating for visitors to observe the Shaker worship.

Watervliet's second Meetinghouse was built in 1848. Its highlights include a two-storey meeting room, and benches at one end for the World's people. It is the only large-scale Shaker Meetinghouse that retains its original interior features.

This date stone is located on the east side of Hancock's Brick Dwelling. Many Shaker buildings include a date stone somewhere in the foundation or in the upper floors near the roof line.

Shaker Meetinghouses, large or small, were built to house worship services. The buildings are an architectural expression of their faith, as they were constructed with an open floor plan to accommodate dancing or "laboring," as the Shakers sometimes called their worship. The rooms are free from obstruction, and contain light, freestanding benches, which were moved to the sides when the dancing began. The benches that were built in around the perimeter walls or in a tiered fashion at one end of the room spoke to the need for Shakers to attract converts by welcoming people from the World. The colors of the Meetinghouses were

This stereoview depicts the dining room at Hancock's East Family dwelling, about 1870. Note the short-backed Shaker chairs that can be pushed under the table for ease of cleaning.

The Meetinghouse that currently stands at Hancock was built in 1793. It was moved to Hancock from the Shaker community in Shirley, Massachusetts, in 1962.

This stereoview of Watervliet's second Meetinghouse dates from around 1871. Note the village's first Meetinghouse—a Moses Johnson design—in the background.

consistently the same, following one of the *Millennial Laws* of 1845: "The meeting house should be painted white without, and of a bluish shade within."

The Shaker peg rail is a seemingly small functional element that provides the basis for the overall design scheme throughout an entire building. Some confusion has surrounded the peg rail's development. The rail itself is not a Shaker invention, although the use of peg rail to surround a room and outfit an entire building is certainly a trademark of the Shakers.

Noel Vicentini, *Meetinghouse, Church Family, Mount Lebanon, New York,* 1936. Shaker design was identified as worthy of documentation in the mid-1930s. This image is part of a series taken on behalf of the American government as part of the Index of American Design.

Pegs were often referred to as clothes pins, and the peg rail was called a pin board by Believers. This terminology is found throughout Shaker journals and other manuscripts. The terms were misunderstood by later researchers, who erroneously assumed that the Shakers had invented the straight clothes pin, which is used to hang items on a line to dry. The peg rail can accommodate a variety of furniture pieces: cupboards, clocks, sconces, chairs, pie-board racks, pipe racks, and knife boxes. The Shakers designed all of these objects with the

The interior of the Hancock Meetinghouse was restored to its original Prussian blue color using an original Shaker paint recipe.

Noel Vicentini, Meetinghouse, view from sisters' cloak or shoe room into sanctuary, Church Family, Mount Lebanon, New York, 1936. The ubiquitous Shaker peg rail is an icon of their design.

peg rail in mind. It allowed them to eliminate clutter from tabletops, and to clean floors more easily. The peg rail is the foundation for the Shakers' design universe.

Some of the most well-known Shaker furniture innovations are the built-in cupboards and drawers that are installed throughout the buildings at every community. Crafted by the finest woodworkers, these functional elements have come to typify smart Shaker design. Built-ins are essentially large case pieces that are literally built into the walls. This design was more efficient for cleaning purposes, as there was no room for dust and dirt to settle either on top or underneath. In the 1816 *Testimonies*, Mother Ann said, "There is no dirt in heaven." This served as a reminder to all Believers that they should strive to keep their living and working quarters as clean as possible, as their villages were meant to represent heaven on earth.

Many built-ins as well as the woodwork in Shaker buildings were originally painted with bright colors. As tastes changed

In the kitchen of the Brick Dwelling at Hancock, several different objects are shown hanging from the peg rail.

with the Victorian era and stripped-down wood with visible grains became popular, the Shakers began to strip the color off their furniture and woodwork. The Shakers often responded to the changing tastes of the times, and did not want to appear backwards to potential converts. For this same reason, they renovated several buildings in the Victorian style in the late 1880s and early 1890s. The Hancock Trustees' Office is one example of this modernization movement among the Shakers.

The objects that the Shakers made speak to their sense of innovation, as well as to their spiritual goals. They were simple, utilitarian objects, which were also made and used by many early Americans. For the Believers, objects were necessary for life, but they were also items that were an extension of a spiritual journey. If your main goal in life was to live what the Shakers would call the Christ-life, every object you created could achieve perfection.

This bright yellow pail is a common utilitarian object, but unique Shaker elements set it apart from its nineteenth-century, worldly counterparts. The color alone is decidedly Shaker. Chrome yellow, as it is called, was often used by

Left: Built-in cupboards and drawers were often painted in bright red lead or chrome yellow washes. This example is located in the Brick Dwelling at Hancock.

Right: The Shakers at Hancock had a large but simple Trustees' Office. It was originally constructed in 1818, with an addition built in 1852.

After a significant renovation in 1895, the Hancock Trustees' Office was more in keeping with Victorian tastes of the World. This allowed the Shakers to put forth a modern face to visitors and potential converts.

Believers to paint furniture, architectural woodwork, and a variety of other objects. The simple bail handle on the pail is rounded underneath just slightly, but enough to bring comfort to the hand of the carrier. This small design detail on a common object took more time to produce than a flat bentwood handle, but for the Shakers, it was a detail that could ease the workload for a Believer in a small but meaningful way.

The throne is a unique piece of furniture—even for the Shakers—and was built for an aging sister at Mount Lebanon. The throne is a platform that raised her up, and allowed her to look out the window at her favorite view of the Lebanon Valley. There is just enough room for a chair and a sewing desk, so that she could sit without being idle, as even aging brethren and sisters were expected to work. And in true Shaker fashion, a drawer was added underneath for storage so that no space was wasted.

Large trestle tables were constructed by the Shakers to seat their communal families in the dwelling house dining rooms. Meals were eaten in silence so that Believers could appreciate the bounty, which God had provided. Brethren and sisters were seated on opposite sides of the dining rooms. Believers were also required to "Shaker their plates"—to clear them—so that no food was wasted. The length of these tables illustrates the ideal of communal living.

The Shakers refined the common bentwood pantry box into a product so well made that many scholars believe they must have developed it. In the nineteenth century, most wooden pantry boxes were made with a straight overlapping joint. This construction did not take into account the swelling and contracting of the wood, which was caused by changing temperatures and humidity levels. This natural movement of the wood caused many boxes to crack and break. The innovative Shaker craftsmen used an oval shape and a special swallowtail joint, so-called because it looked like the tail of a bird. These laps, sometimes called fingers, reached around the side of the box and were tacked into place. The shape of the swallowtails allowed for the wood to expand and contract and greatly reduced the amount of cracking, thus extending the life of the box. This design detail made for a better box, and the Shakers at Mount Lebanon, along with a few other Shaker villages, made oval box production into a successful industry.

This chrome yellow pail was made at the Mount Lebanon Shaker community in the nineteenth century. "Harriet G. Augusta" is written on the bottom in pencil. Cooperage was a large-scale activity at Mount Lebanon.

This throne is a unique piece of Shaker furniture. It was specifically crafted for an aging sister by a fellow Believer.

This 20-foot trestle table was made at Mount Lebanon around 1830.

Right: This clock was made by Brother Isaac Newton Youngs at Mount Lebanon in 1840. It is designed to be hung from the peg rail, and features a bright, chrome-yellow wash inside the case.

Bottom right: These colorful oval boxes were made at the Mount Lebanon community around 1840. They were made in a variety of sizes, and typically maple was used for the sides and pine for the tops.

Shakers kept clocks in several rooms throughout their dwelling houses and workshops, and many Shaker brothers were skilled clockmakers. The Shakers, ever practical and measured, were very concerned with keeping track of time, perhaps more so than their worldly counterparts. Time for them was an earthly concern; however, each tick of the clock moved a Believer a little closer to death and departure from this present realm. Only then would they experience the release of their soul into heaven, which is the ultimate goal of any Shaker. This concept of time was stated best by Brother Isaac

Newton Youngs of Mount Lebanon, who made several clocks during his lifetime. He inscribed this poem inside the case of one of his clocks in 1840: "O Time! How swift that solemn day rolls on, when from these mortal scenes we shall be gone!!!" The Shakers meant to live their lives on earth to the fullest, perfecting each moment and each object in God's image, before they would find release and peace in heaven.

Despite the many inventions accurately credited to Shaker ingenuity, recent research has revealed that the group has been credited with several inventions that they did not devise. Objects such as the circular saw, the straight clothes pin, and the washing machine among others are not, in fact, Shaker inventions. In these and several other cases, the Shakers improved upon an existing object, often making it better than the original. This resulted in the Shakers receiving credit for the invention.

Noel Vicentini, *Broom Shop, West Family, Watervliet, New York,* 1936. Watervliet, Mount Lebanon, and Hancock were all photographically documented as part of the American government project, the Index of American Design.

One invention that Believers are likely responsible for is the flat broom. Since brooms were first utilized, bunches of twigs, straw, or broomcorn were tied together in a bundle and used to sweep out debris. Brother Theodore Bates (1762–1846) at the Watervliet community invented a vise to hold the broomcorn bristles flat so that they could be stitched across with twine. The resulting shape made for a more efficient broom, which soon became a standard household item. The Shakers marketed and sold a variety of brooms and brushes, and almost every community participated in this lucrative trade.

In each Shaker dwelling house, the upper floors were mainly reserved for bedrooms, or retiring rooms as the Shakers referred to them. Several Believers would share the same retiring room. With many beds in each room, it was essential that they could be moved easily for cleaning.

Shaker brooms were another high-quality product that many villages produced. The labels shown here were attached to brooms made at Mount Lebanon.

Therefore, Shaker beds often had rollers on the feet, and were constructed out of lighter woods to allow the sisters to move them, and make cleaning the retiring rooms more efficient. A variety of paint colors brightened the rooms, and beds were no exception. In the Shakers' *Millennial Laws* of 1845, it was required that "bedsteads should be painted green—comforters should be of a modest color" although no reason was given for this directive. In Shaker collections today, many beds retain a chrome-green paint layer.

Several Shaker objects reveal the innovative, functional, and spiritual nature of their makers. They have a lasting impact that resonates for people. The object itself becomes more recognizable than the religious movement that inspired its initial creation. Above all, these objects were made to be useful and used. They were made for people, as gifts that might serve to ease their burdens, and make their lives and work a bit easier. "I almost expect to be remembered as a chair," said Sister Mildred Barker, at Sabbathday Lake in 1984, in her interview in the Ken Burn's film, *The Shakers*. Shaker material culture represents the memories of individuals, as well as a movement that continues to inspire designers in today's modern world.

This green bed is on display in the 1830 Brick Dwelling at Hancock. Note the rollers on each leg, making the bed easier to move for cleaning.

DECLINE OF THE SHAKERS

MANY FACTORS HAVE contributed to the Shakers' dwindling numbers since their peak in the mid-nineteenth century. One common misconception is that the number of Shakers declined due to the practice of celibacy. While this belief certainly does not help the group's numbers, it is not the primary reason there are so few Shakers today. In the nineteenth century, the Shakers took in many children from orphanages and foundling hospitals. Parents who could not afford to feed their children sometimes indentured them to the Shakers. These children were housed in separate buildings from the adult Shakers, and were referred to as the Children's Order. They had assigned caretakers for each gender, and were well cared for, educated, and learned a trade that would benefit them in the World should they choose to leave the Shaker community when they came of age.

In the late nineteenth century, orphanages began to seek out smaller home environments for their charges rather than institutional settings. The early twentieth century saw the Children's Order closed at most of the communities that remained open. Older sisters and brethren who were caretakers began to leave or pass away, and fewer parents left children with the Shakers once they were no longer seen as viable options and thriving communities. Although the Shakers believed that children would increase their numbers, in the end, very few of these children chose to stay and sign the Shaker covenant making them lifelong Believers.

Girls and their caretakers at the North Family of Shakers in Enfield, Connecticut, about 1897. The hand gestures of the subjects reflect the fondness between the sisters and the girls in their care.

The changing economic and religious climate in the second half of the nineteenth century was almost certainly the main reason for the decline in converts to Shaker communities. Rural America was based on an agrarian economy, where farming was common. The Shakers ran large-scale farming operations, and many people who joined were already knowledgeable about that way of life. With the coming of the railroad and the Industrial Revolution, the previously known ways of life began to change. The shift from an agrarian to an industrial society, and the changing social mindset that came with this shift, was detrimental for the Shakers and their villages. The Shakers embraced the railroads and even allowed station depots to be built on their land. They understood that they could use the railroads to transport their products to an even wider audience. However, the same railroads that served to benefit the Shakers also hurt them. The coming of the railroads meant progress, opening up new frontiers in the west, and turning cities into industrial centers.

The opportunities for unskilled laborers in the new factories were large draws for young men and women during this time. Shaker villages had been places of refuge for unwed mothers and widows who could not navigate society on their own, but factories now gave these women jobs and an income independent of a husband, and they could live on their own in the growing cities of America.

In a changing religious climate, fewer people needed the sanctuary of Shaker villages where they were guaranteed salvation by living a Christ-like life. As more people became literate, they were less dependent on another's interpretation of the Bible, and could make more informed decisions on their own. The ideas behind communal religious societies no longer appealed to a populace who could make their own way in the world, and did not have to rely on spiritual guidance alone.

Image of West Pittsfield railroad station, also known as Shaker Depot, about 1925. The station was built on land donated for this purpose by the East Family at Hancock.

SHAKERS TODAY

THE UNITED SOCIETY of Believers in Christ's Second Appearing is America's longest-lived communal society. The last community at Sabbathday Lake, Maine, continues to be a thriving spiritual center and a place that accepts novitiates interested in living the Christ-life. For more than two hundred years, outsider accounts have spoken of the Shakers' demise, yet they are still among us. There are two sisters and one brother currently living the Shaker life.

The Shaker *Testimonies* of 1816 recount the story: "Not long after the opening of the gospel at Watervliet, Mother Ann was speaking to a large number of the Believers, concerning those who were called by the gospel, and of their bearing and travailing for other souls, and she said, 'If there is but one called out of a generation, and that soul is faithful, it will have to travail and bear for all its generation; for the world will be redeemed by generations.'"

Perhaps this will be the generation where more than one soul joins the Shakers, and the Believers today continue to hope. However, the remaining Shakers are also realists and have said that if it is God's will that the Shaker faith ends with them, then they are ready to accept that eventuality. They welcome visitors to Sunday Meeting and hope that people of the World will be inspired by their message and better understand their faith.

They continue the Shaker practice of embracing technology, using websites and email correspondence to communicate

The Meetinghouse at the Sabbathday Lake Shaker Village in New Gloucester, Maine, was built in 1794.

with the world around them, and making people aware of their lives and their message. They are actively involved in educational outreach through the museum and library, and hold several festivals each year that celebrate music, Native American heritage in the area, and Shaker scholarship. Though they are few in number they continue to work the land: raising sheep and cattle, making culinary herbs and herbal teas, and harvesting apples from their extensive orchards in the fall. They have an active group of international supporters, called the Friends of the Shakers, which helps to preserve and promote the livelihood of Sabbathday Lake Shaker Village for future generations.

Aerial view of Sabbathday Lake Shaker Village, 2007.

PLACES TO VISIT

Canterbury Shaker Village, 288 Shaker Road, Canterbury, NH 03224. Telephone: 001 603 783 9511. Website: www.shakers.org

Enfield Shaker Museum, 447 NH Route 4A, Enfield, NH 03748. Telephone: 001 603 632 4346. Website: www.shakermuseum.org

Alfred Shaker Museum, 118 Shaker Hill Road, Alfred, ME 04002. Telephone: 001 207 324 8669. Website: www.alfredshakermuseum.com

Hancock Shaker Village, 1843 West Housatonic Street, Pittsfield, MA 01201. Telephone: 001 413 443 0188. Website: www.hancockshakervillage.org

Sabbathday Lake Shaker Village, 707 Shaker Rd, New Gloucester, ME 04260. Telephone: 001 207 926 4597. Website: www.shaker.lib.me.us

Pleasant Hill Shaker Village, 3501 Lexington Road Harrodsburg, KY 40330. Telephone: 001 800 734 5611. Website: www.shakervillageky.org

Shaker Museum at South Union, 850 Shaker Museum Road, Auburn, KY 42206. Telephone: 001 270 542 4167. Website: www.shakermuseum.com

Shaker Museum – Mount Lebanon, 202 Shaker Road, New Lebanon, NY 12125. Telephone: 001 518 794 9100. Website: www.shakermuseumandlibrary.org

Shaker Heritage Society, 875 Watervliet Shaker Road, Albany, NY 12211. Telephone: 001 518 456 7890. Website: www.shakerheritage.org

Friends of White Water Shaker Village, 11813 Oxford Road, Harrison, OH 45030. Telephone: 001 513 738 5928. Website: www.whitewatervillage.org

Shaker Historical Society and Museum, 16740 South Park Boulevard, Shaker Heights, OH 44120. Telephone: 001 216 921 1201. Website: www.shakerhistoricalsociety.org

Fruitlands Museum, 102 Prospect Hill Road, Harvard, MA
01451. Telephone: 001 978 456 3924.
Website: www.fruitlands.org

The Metropolitan Museum of Art, 1000 Fifth Avenue, New
York, NY 10028. Telephone: 001 212 535 7710.
Website: www.metmuseum.org

Philadelphia Museum of Art, 2600 Benjamin Franklin
Parkway, Philadelphia, PA 19130. Telephone: 001 215
763 8100. Website: www.philamuseum.org

Winterthur Museum, Garden and Library, 5105 Kennett
Pike, Wilmington, DE 19735. Telephone: 001 800 448
3883. Website: www.winterthur.org

In the United Kingdom:

The American Museum in Britain, Claverton Manor, Bath,
BA2 7BD. Telephone: 44 1225 460503.
Website: www.americanmuseum.org

FURTHER READING

Boyce, Martha, Dale Covington, and Richard Spence. *Maps of the Shaker West; A Journey of Discovery.* Knot Garden Press, 1997.

Carr, Sister Frances. *Growing up Shaker.* United Society of Shakers, 1995.

——*Shaker Your Plate: Of Shaker Cooks and Cooking.* United Society of Shakers, 1985.

Crosthwaite, Jane F. *The Shaker Spiritual Notices of Eleanor Potter.* Richard W. Couper Press, Hamilton College Library, 2013.

Emlen, Robert P. *Shaker Village Views.* University Press of New England, 1987.

Goodwillie, Christian, and M. Stephen Miller. *Handled with Care: The Function of Form in Shaker Craft.* Hancock Shaker Village, 2006.

Grant, Jerry V., and Douglas R. Allen. *Shaker Furniture Makers.* (Hancock Shaker Village.) University Press of New England, 1989.

Hadd, Brother Arnold. "Agreeable to Our Understanding: The Shaker Covenant." *Shaker Quarterly* 24 (1996): 87, 109.

Herzberg, Lesley. *A Promising Venture: Shaker Photographs from the WPA.* American Communal Societies Series; No. 7. Richard W. Couper Press, Hamilton College Library, 2012.

Kirk, John T. *The Shaker World: Art, Life, Belief.* Harry N. Abrams, 1997.

Koomler, Sharon Duane. *Seen and Received: The Shakers' Private Art.* Hancock Shaker Village, 2000.

Medlicott, Carol. *Issachar Bates: A Shaker's Journey.* University Press of New England, 2013.

Miller, Amy Bess, and Persis Fuller, eds. *The Best of Shaker Cooking.* Rev. Macmillan Publ. Co., 1985.

Miller, Amy Bess. *Shaker Medicinal Herbs: A Compendium of History, Lore, and Uses.* Storey Books, 1998.

Miller, M. Stephen. *Inspired Innovations: A Celebration of Shaker Ingenuity.* University Press of New England, 2010.

Nicoletta, Julie, and Bret Morgan. *The Architecture of the Shakers.* The Countryman Press, 1995.

Paterwic, Stephen J. *Historical Dictionary of the Shakers.* Historical Dictionaries of Religions, Philosophies, and Movements; No. 87. Scarecrow Press, Inc., 2008.

Patterson, Daniel W. *Gift Drawing and Gift Song: A Study of Two Forms of Shaker Inspiration.* United Society of Shakers, 1983.

Rieman, Timothy D. *The Encyclopedia of Shaker Furniture.* Schiffer Publishing, 2003.

Sanchez, Anita. *Mr. Lincoln's Chair: The Shakers and Their Quest for Peace.* The McDonald & Woodward Publ. Co., 2009.

Stein, Stephen J. *The Shaker Experience in America.* Yale University, 1992.

Stiles, Lauren A. *Shaker "Great Barns" 1820s–1880s: Evolution of Shaker Dairy Barn Design and its Relation to the Agricultural Press.* Richard W. Couper Press, Hamilton College Library, 2013.

Thorne-Thomsen, Kathleen. *Shaker Children: True Stories and Crafts. 2 Biographies and 30 Activities.* Chicago Review Press, Inc., 1996.

Wergland, Glendyne R., ed. *Visiting the Shakers 1778–1849.* Richard W. Cooper Press. American Communal Societies Series; No. 1, 2007.

———ed. *Visiting the Shakers 1850–1899.* Richard W. Cooper Press. American Communal Societies Series; No. 2, 2010.

———ed. *Sisters in the Faith: Shaker Women and Equality of the Sexes.* University of Massachusetts Press, 2011.

Williams, Stephen Guion. *A Place in Time: The Shakers at Sabbathday Lake, Maine.* David R. Godine, 2006.

INDEX

References to images are in *italic*.

Advertising labels 33, 34
Andrews, Edward and Faith 29
Ann Lee 4, 5
Ann Lee, A Biography 7
Apostate 17
Architecture 41
Barns, bank 41
Baptists 9
Barker, Sr. Mildred 54
Bates, Eldr. Betsy 18
Bates, Br. Theodore 53
Bible 16, 57
Bishop, Eld. Rufus 6
Boxes: oval/round 31, *31*; bentwood pantry 51
Brainard, D. C. *34*
Brick Dwelling, Hancock 15, 27, 43, 44, 54
Broadsides *33*, 35
Brooms 53, *54*
Built-ins 48: cupboards 49
Camisards 4
Caretakers 55, *56*
Carriers *31, 38*
Catalogs 35
Celibacy 5, 55
Chairs *29*: catalogs *36*; factory 35; ladder back 35, seating/cane, splint, webbing 35; short-backed 45; showroom 35; tilter *34*
Children's Order 55
Christ-life 49, 57, 58
Christ spirit 13, 17
Church Family 14, 44
Church of England 4
Civil War 16
Cloak business 38: cloaks 32, 38, *39*; Dorothy 39
Clocks *52*
Cohoon, Sr. Hannah *7*, 22
Collins, Sr. Polly 6, *7*, 22, 23
Colors 45: bright red lead *49*; chrome yellow 49
Communal-living 13, 28: property 13; religious societies 57
Communities 43, 56
Confession 13
Cooperage 51: pail, chrome yellow *51*
Covenant 13
Dance *18*, 19
Day of Judgment 9
Delcheff, Sr. Anna *39*
Design 33, 34
Dining room, Hancock *45*
Doolittle, Eldr. Antoinette 14
"Dual Godhead" 13, 23

Durgin, Eldr. Dorothy 39
Dwelling Houses 43, *44*, 53
Elders/Eldresses 11, 13, 14
An Emblem of the Heavenly Sphere 7, *12*, 23
Equality 13
"Era of Manifestations" 20, 21, 22
Evans, Eld. Fredrick W. 7, 14
Fancy goods 37
"Feast ground" 21
"First Parents" 10
"Fountain stone" *21, 22*
French Prophets 4
Friends of the Shakers 59
Garden seed industry 32
Gender cooperation 38
"Gift drawings" 21–3: Guardian Angel 23; Parting of Red Sea 23
Goodrich, Eld. Daniel Jr. 32
"Gospel order" 14
Green Gage plums 34
Hancock, MA 7, 15, 19, 21, 22, 27, 32, 33, 37, 39, 41, 46, 47, 49, 50, 54: East Family 45, 57
"Harriet G. Augusta", Sr. [Stone] 51
"Holy Mount" 21
Hymnals 19
Indentures 55
Index of American Design 47, 53
Industrial Revolution 56
Innovation 31, 41, 48, 49, 51
Instruments 18, 21, 22
Inventions 53
Jacobs, Sr. Clarissa 39
Jesus Christ 23
Johnson, Br. Moses 44, 46
Labels *36*, 54
Laboring 6, 45
Lamson, David R. 17
Manchester, England 4, 7
Mariah 8
Marketing 31
Meacham, Father Joseph 10
Meeting Houses 14, 18, 44, 45, *46, 47*, 48, *59*: colors 45–6
Methodists 4, 5
Millennial Church 13
Millennial Laws 11, 46, 54
Millennial Praises 20
Ministry 10, *14*, 31, 44
Mother Ann 5, 7, 8, 9, 13, 20, 22, 23, 27, 58: grave *11*
Mother Ann Lee 6, 10, 23
"Mother's Work" 20
Mount Lebanon, NY 3, 10, 18, 31, 32, 33, 34, 35, 44, 50, 52: North Family 14; South Family 35; Chair Factory 35
Mountain Meeting *21*
Music 19, *21*
Neale, Emma J. *38*, 39
New Gloucester, ME 59
Niskayuna (Niskeyuna) 8, 9, 10

Novitiates 13, 58
Office Deacons 31
Offord, Eld. Daniel 14
Oval boxes 31, 52: production 51
Patents *34, 39*
Pacifism 9, 16
"Parent Ministry" 10, 16
Peg rail 46–8, *48*, 52
Poplarware *38*
Products for sale 31
Quakers 4, 5
Railroads 56–7: station *57*
Reed, Sr. Polly Jane 25, *26–7*
Revolutionary War 9, 16
Rockers *36*
Round Stone Barn 41–3, *42, 43*
Sabbathday Lake, ME 54, 58: Shaker Village *59*
Seed-boxes, lists *33*
Seed packets/papers *32*, 33: routes 33
Sewing boxes *38*
Shaking Quakers 5
Shirley, MA 22, 32, 46
Simple Gifts 20
Sisters 15, 43, 56
Sisters' Dairy/Weave shop 15; shop, Hancock *37*
Spinning wheels 26, 27, *30*
Spiritual gifts 21: names 20–1; trance 16; revelations 25
Sunday Meeting 58
Swallowtail joint *51*
Terry, Eld. David 32
Testimonies 6, 13, 27, 28, 48, 58
Trade Mark *36*
The Tree of Life 22
The Tree of Light or Blazing Tree 7
Trustees 16, 31, 33, *35*, 36: Office 37, *49, 50*
Two Years' Experience Among Shakers 17, 21
A Type of Mother Hannah's Pocket Handkerchief 25
United Society of Believers in Christ's Second Appearing 4, 8, 10, 11, 17, 18, 20, 22, 41, 43, 58
Victorian style 49, 50: tastes 34
Visions 4
Wagan, Eld. Robert M. *35*, 36
Wardley, James and Jane 4: Society 4
Watervliet, NY 8, 11, 32, 33, 44, 45, 46, 53, 58: West Family *53*
Wells, Seth Youngs 6
The Whirling Gift 6, 17
White, Eldr. Anna 14
Whittaker, Father James 7, 10, 23
Woodwork *40*, 41
Wooden carriers 38
The "World" 14, 18, 31, 58
Wright, Mother Lucy 10
Worship 16
Yarn swift *30*
Youngs, Br. Isaac Newton 52–3